SPECIAL FORCES

SPECIAL FORCES

John Farndon

Consultant: Dr Gregory Fremont-Barnes

Miles Kelly

First published in 2010 by Miles Kelly Publishing Ltd
Harding's Barn, Bardfield End Green, Thaxted, Essex, CM6 3PX, UK

This edition printed 2014

6 8 10 9 7 5

Publishing Director Belinda Gallagher
Creative Director Jo Cowan
Managing Editor Rosie Neave
Assistant Editor Claire Philip
Volume Designer Simon Lee
Junior Designer Kayleigh Allen
Image Manager Liberty Newton
Indexer Gill Lee
Production Manager Elizabeth Collins
Reprographics Anthony Cambray, Stephan Davis, Ian Paulyn
Assets Lorraine King

ISBN 978-1-84810-283-5

Printed in China

British Library Cataloguing-in-Publication Data
A catalogue record for this book is available from the British Library

ACKNOWLEDGEMENTS
The publishers would like to thank the following artists who have contributed to this book:

Julian Baker (JB Illustrations), Oliver Frey (Temple Rogers), Alex Pang, Mike White (Temple Rogers)

All other artworks are from the Miles Kelly Artwork Bank

The publishers would like to thank the following sources for the use of their photographs:

t = top, b = bottom, l = left, r = right, c = centre, m = main, bg = background, f = far

Alamy 8(tl) World History Archive, 23(br) A. T. Willett, 25(br) Imagestate Media Partners Limited – Impact Photos **Corbis** 12(br), 15(bl) Bettmann, 18(cl) Patrick Ward, 19(cl), 21(tr) Hulton-Deutsch Collection, 22(b) JP Laffont/Sygma, 23(t) Lance Iversen/San Francisco Chronicle, 29(m) Reuters, 34(m) Third Eye Images, 36(m) Third Eye Images, 37(br) HO/Reuters, 38(c) Louie Psihoyos, (b) Jim Sugar, 42(m), 43(tl) Ed Quinn, 43(b) Ed Darack/Science Faction, 45(b) Brian Snyder/Reuters **Dreamstime** 28(bl) Fotokate, 39(tbg) Irochka **Fotolia** 14(tl) Samantha Grandy, 18–19(b) Thaut Images **Getty Images** 11(br), 16(tr) Popperfoto, 20(b), 30(m), 31(tl), 31(br), 35(tm) MILpictures by Tom Weber, 39(tr) Stocktrek Images, 40(r) Time & Life Pictures, 44–45(tc) **iStockphoto** 12(l) ChuckSchugPhotography, 13(bfr) DoctorQ, 14–15(t) Rockfinder, 15(br) Richcano, 16–17(bc) Mettus, 17(tl) Linda Steward, 18(bl) Duncan1890, 20–21(bc) SpxChrome, 22-23(tc) Liliboas, 26(tl) Jane, 28(bg) AndreasG, 32(tl) Krakozawr, 32(bl) Ollikainen, 34(cr) Makhnach/Macsek, 18(t) 2ndLookGraphics, 42–43 (bg) Dinn, 42(tr) Axstokes, 44–45(bg) Foundation7 **Moviestore Collection** 46–47(m) Revolution Studios **Rex** 13(br), 21(b) Bournemouth News, 24–25(b) Dmitry Beliakov, 25(tl) Action Press, 26–27(m) Sipa Press, 35(tl), 39(b) Greg E. Mathieson, 40(l) Sipa Press **TopFoto.co.uk** 6–7 Â©RIA Novosti, 14(tr), 14–15(bc) Â©2006 Alinari, 46(tr) The Granger Collection/New York

Every effort has been made to acknowledge the source and copyright holder of each picture. Miles Kelly Publishing apologises for any unintentional errors or omissions.

Made with paper from a sustainable forest

www.mileskelly.net
info@mileskelly.net

CONTENTS

WHAT ARE SPECIAL FORCES?

i Special forces are small groups of carefully selected soldiers. They are highly trained and their task is to go on secret and dangerous missions. For example, they could be ordered to make a daring attack on a target deep inside enemy territory (land). Today they play a vital role in the fight against terrorism.

▲ There's often no time on a special forces mission to stop in a nice, dry place. Here, Russian Spetsnaz soldiers jump from their moving Armoured Personal Carrier straight into the water, with guns at the ready.

BANDS OF HEROES

◀ This 5th to 6th century BC frieze in the palace of the Persian King Darius at Susa shows the Immortals.

2 The Immortals were the elite troops of the Persian Empire in the 6th century BC. They were called Immortals because it was thought that there were always exactly 10,000 of them. Any soldier who was killed or badly wounded was at once replaced by a highly trained reserve. Immortals carried spears with silver handles and wore coats made of metal scales beneath their robes.

3 The Spartans were a warrior people who fought in ancient Greece. Spartan soldiers were renowned for their toughness and lived on only the bare necessities. Today the word 'spartan' means stern, disciplined and without luxury.

4 A band of just 300 Spartan soldiers, led by King Leonidas, fought a heroic last stand at the Battle of Thermopylae in 480 BC. Thermopylae was a narrow pass and its name means 'hot gates'. With just a few hundred others, the Spartans held the pass for seven days against a Persian army that may have numbered more than 100,000. However they were all killed, eventually.

▼ An artist's impression of how the Spartans might have looked as they braced themselves for their heroic stand against the might of Persia at Thermopylae in 480 BC.

◀ The highest officials in the Roman Empire were always protected by the tough soldiers of the Praetorian Guard, shown here wearing blue and orange.

5 The Praetorian Guard were the Roman emperor's personal bodyguard.

They were set up by Emperor Augustus in 31 BC to protect him from being murdered, as his father Julius Caesar was. Their symbol was a scorpion. The Guard became more and more powerful and ruthless. In the end, they actually assassinated emperors if they did not approve of them, rather than protecting them. So for centuries, the Guard decided who became emperor.

Iron helmet

Round shield

Axe

Mail shirt

◀ In 11th century Byzantium, no one messed with the fierce Viking soldiers of the Varangian Guard, who fought with huge axes.

▶ Varangian sword, 9th century Russia

6 The Varangian Guard were Viking warriors who protected an emperor.

Byzantium was a vast empire centred on modern Istanbul that lasted for 1100 years, from the 4th to the 15th century. In the 11th century, the Emperor Basil brought in rough, tough Viking warriors from Russia to be his guard. They fought only with axes and were loyal to no one but each other. The most famous of them was Harald Hardrada, who died trying to conquer England in 1066.

SWORDS AND HORSES

7 The Knights Templar were an order (group) of Christian knights that is now surrounded by legend. They were set up by nine knights in 1119 to protect pilgrims visiting the Holy Land (Palestine), and named for their base at Temple Mount in Jerusalem. The Templars became wealthy and powerful, but caused resentment among rival orders. On Friday 13 October, 1307, the order was disbanded by the Pope.

▶ Templar knights were famous for their courage and skill with swords.

8 Ninja were Japanese warriors with amazing skills who fought with katana (curved swords). Often pictured in black tunics and masks, they usually travelled in disguise. Their task was to sneak into enemy territory to identify weak defences, set fire to enemy castles and assassinate enemy leaders. Ninja equipment included special ropes and hooks for scaling castle walls.

9 The Ninja were so secretive and skilled that people thought they must be magical. Some stories say that they could cause enemies to become rooted to the spot with a touch of their hand. It was also believed that they could fly on kites, become invisible and change into animals.

▲ Ninjas could climb so swiftly and silently that people said they must be able to fly into enemy castles.

A Templar Knight is truly a fearless knight, and secure on every side, for his soul is protected by the armour of faith, just as his body is protected by the armour of steel.

St Bernard de Clairvaux (1135)

▶ Few soldiers have ever been more glamorous than the Korean flower knights who went into battle wearing make-up and beautiful silk robes.

10 The Hwarang were the flower knights of 8th century Silla in Korea. They were probably called 'flower knights' because they were young noblemen who wore make-up and very flowery robes. Famed for their extraordinary skill with swords and for never retreating in battle, the Hwarang were also inspired by the spiritual teachers Confucius and Buddha. The most famous Hwarang was Kim Yu-Shin, who unified Korea in the 8th century.

11 Cossacks were warriors from southern Ukraine and Russia, known for their courage and horsemanship. Boys born into Cossack communities were rocked to sleep with war songs rather than lullabies, and taught to ride as soon as they could walk. They boasted that 100 Cossack horsemen were quieter than a single ordinary soldier. In the 18th century they became the Russian emperor's 'eyes', looking out for signs of trouble.

◀ The Cossacks of Russia were famed for their supreme horsemanship and their toughness – and also for their wild parties.

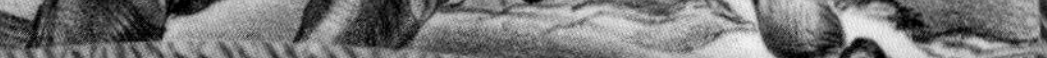

SCOUTS AND RAIDERS

12 American Indian dog soldiers made sure they fought to the last. Every year, four soldiers were chosen to wear a length of leather called the dog-rope. During battle each soldier attached the free end of his rope to the ground, pinning himself to the spot, and would not free himself until his comrades were safe. The dog soldiers led the last fight of the Cheyenne people against the American settlers in the mid-1800s.

▶ Dog soldiers wore huge, distinctive headdresses, which they made by sticking bird feathers into their caps.

13 For the US cavalry, American Indian scouts were the unsung heroes of the Indian Wars in the 19th century. These were a series of conflicts between the US government and the American Indians. In 1860 the president authorized the US cavalry to take on 1000 American Indians as scouts (guides). The scouts' inside knowledge of the land and their targets made them a highly effective weapon for the cavalry.

▲ In their fight against the American Indians, the US cavalry relied on American Indian scouts such as these five Apaches, who were renowned for their uncanny tracking ability.

◀ The raids made by small bands of Confederates in the American Civil War inspired legends.

14 During the American Civil War (1861–1865), legends were inspired by raiding parties. These were groups of men sent by the Confederate army to attack towns deep within the territory of the opposing Unionists. The most famous was Morgan's Raid in 1863, when the raiding party rode 1600 kilometres in 46 days. They did a great deal of damage, but few came back alive. One who did was 'Stovepipe' Johnson, who had led an earlier raid to capture the town of Newburgh, Indiana, in 1862.

15 The Lovat Scouts have been described as 'half-wolf, half-jackrabbit'. They were formed in 1900 to carry out raids and observation for the British in the Boer War (1899–1902). Some learnt their skills as ghillies (hunting guides) in the Scottish mountains. They sometimes wore ghillie suits (body camouflage) and many were crack shots. The Lovat Scouts later became the first sniper units. Snipers are sharpshooters who fire on their targets from hidden positions.

▶ A pair of Lovat scouts, wearing their 'ghillie' camouflage suits, take part in a training exercise.

QUICK-FIRE QUIZ

1. How many dog soldiers wore the dog-rope each year?
2. What is a ghillie suit?
3. Who led the raid that captured the town of Newburgh in 1862?

Answers:
1. Four 2. A form of body camouflage 3. 'Stovepipe' Johnson

WORLD WAR I

16 The US Army Corps of Signals was the first specialist communications force. The armies of World War I (1914–1918) had to keep in touch over vast distances and quickly pass on information about enemy activity. When the USA entered World War I (1917), the US Army Corps of Signals developed the first radiotelephones so commanders could talk directly by radio on the battlefield.

▲ US Army Signal Corps, shown here in 1918 with their field telephone. Its development enabled commanders to talk directly to each other on the battlefield for the first time.

▼ An aerial photo taken from an airship in May 1916 during World War I.

► During World War I, a co-pilot would lean out of the open cockpit of his scouting plane to drop bombs on enemy targets by hand.

17 Spying from the air was the task of reconnaissance units. During the French Revolutionary Wars (1792–1802), the French used hot-air balloons to spy on their enemies, but it was in World War I that aerial reconnaissance (observation from the air) really took off. Some missions were in planes, with a pilot and an observer. At first, the observers drew pictures but later cameras were used. In some cases, an observer had to dangle on a rope far below an airship hidden in the clouds!

18 The Italian Arditi may have been the first modern special force. Formed in 1917, their task was to make breaks in enemy defences before major attacks. Their name comes from the Italian for 'daring' and they relied on speed, timing and the element of surprise. Their weapons included anything from machine guns to flamethrowers, but Arditi were often seen with daggers between their teeth ready for hand-to-hand combat, and a bag of hand-grenades for creating panic in the enemy.

▼ Fast moving 'shock troops' such as these German stormtroopers might catch the enemy by surprise and so break through enemy defences.

▲ The Italian Arditi were feared for their swift and ruthless surprise attacks as they pounced on the enemy with knives and hand-grenades.

19 Units of German stormtroopers stormed (broke through) enemy lines to weaken them in preparation for major attacks. Nowadays such units are called shock troops or fireteams. They are daring, fast-moving, lightly armed soldiers who catch the enemy by surprise with fast raids.

TRUE OR FALSE?

1. The USA entered World War I in 1918.
2. Arditi forces used flamethrowers.
3. Fireteams carry heavy weapons.
4. World War I saw the first use of radiotelephones.
5. The French Revolutionary Wars ended in 1802.

Answers:
1. False – they entered in 1917 2. True
3. False – Fireteams are lightly armed
4. True 5. True

WORLD WAR II

20 In World War II (1939–1945), British Prime Minister Winston Churchill created a force called the Commandos. They made daring raids from Britain in enemy-occupied Europe. In 1942 they attacked a dock at the French port of St Nazaire, vital to the Germans for repairing the battleship *Tirpitz*. The British sent a ship packed with explosives to ram the dock gates while the Commandos destroyed the dock facilities.

▲ British Commandos crawl forward under sniper fire during an attack in the last months of World War II. Commandos wore red berets to show enemy soldiers that they were part of an elite force.

▶ David Stirling (in the cap) with soldiers from the Long Range Desert Group that helped him try out ideas for the SAS in the North African desert in 1942.

21 The British Special Air Service (SAS) is the most famous special force. It was set up in North Africa in 1941 by David Stirling, who was nicknamed 'The Phantom Major' because he could slip like a ghost in and out of enemy territory. On their first mission, SAS forces used parachutes for a raid on German airfields in the Sahara, but bad weather blew them off course. After that most raids were high-speed dashes in armed jeeps. The SAS proved so effective that it is the inspiration for all special forces today.

22 With parachutes, special forces could be dropped quickly and quietly into enemy territory.

22 With parachutes, special forces could be dropped quickly and quietly into enemy territory. US Airborne Divisions prepared the ground for the Allied invasion of Normandy, France, in 1944. On the night of 5–6 June, 1944, 13,100 soldiers were dropped inside German-occupied France, with orders to seize and hold vital enemy targets. Each man carried over 32 kilograms of equipment as well as his parachute. They succeeded in spreading confusion behind enemy lines, but many were killed.

1. David [illegible] 'The Ghostly [illegible]
2. The Allies invaded Normandy in 1944.
3. The 'Black Devils' was the French name for the 1st SSF.

Answers:
1. False – his nickname was 'The Phantom Major'
2. True
3. False – this was what the Germans called them

23 The US 1st Special Service Force (SSF) was known by the Germans as the 'Black Devils'. They were famed for capturing 'impossible' targets – climbing cliffs in the dead of night, blackening their faces to make themselves less visible, and knocking out guards silently in hand-to-hand combat. They often caught their enemies so much off-guard that they were able to disarm them without a shot being fired. Wherever they went they left stickers saying *Das dicke Ende kommt noch*, which in German means, 'The worst is yet to come'.

24 Australian coastwatchers played a vital role in the Allied fight against the Japanese in the Pacific Ocean. Their job was to hide alone on Pacific islands, keeping a constant watch on the movements of Japanese forces. They often recruited native people to help, and rescued many troops captured by the Japanese.

▲ In World War II, special forces such as the Commandos became skilled in parachuting behind enemy lines under cover of darkness. It was very dangerous, but helped them catch the enemy by surprise.

JUNGLE KINGS

25 'Better to die than be a coward' is the motto of the Gurkha soldiers of Nepal. They first fought for the British as long ago as 1815, but they became famous in World War II for their skill and bravery in jungle warfare.

▼ The Royal Gurkha rifles, seen here training at The Royal Military Academy Sandhurst in England, are regarded as some of the world's best soldiers.

▲ The sharp, curved blade of the kukri looks lethal, but Gurkhas insist it is used mainly for cooking!

26 A Gurkha always carries a long, curved blade called a kukri. It was said that once a kukri was drawn, it had to taste enemy blood – or the owner would have to cut himself.

▼ This map shows the route taken by the Chindits on their epic raid through Japanese lines in the Burmese jungle in Operation Longcloth.

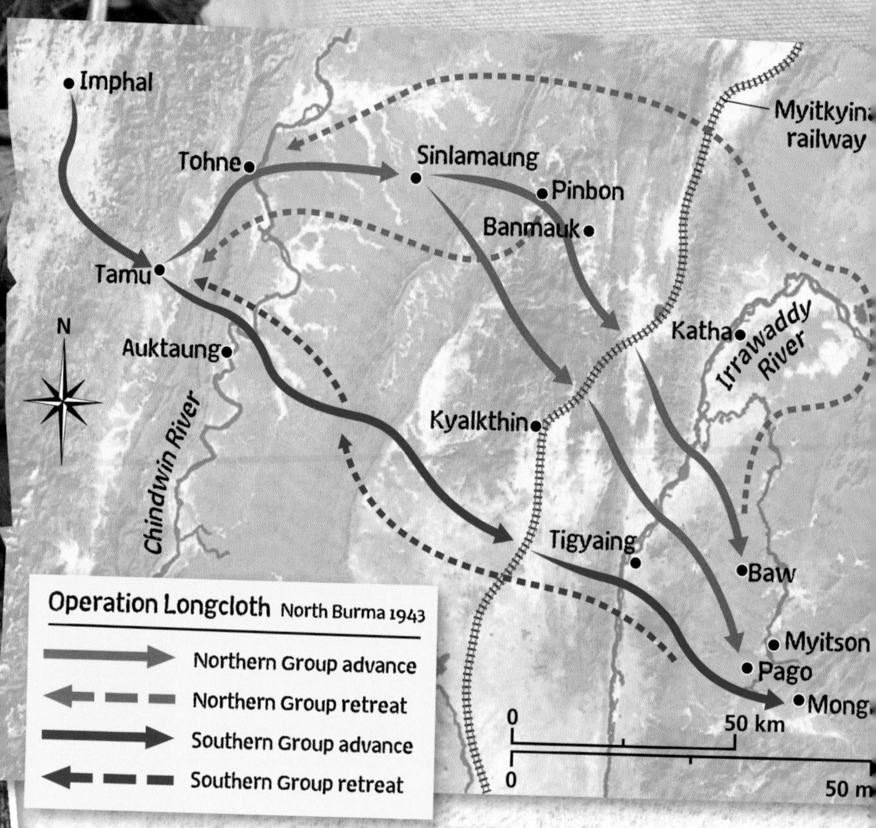

Gurkhas from the British Army on parade in India.

27 The Chindits were Britain's biggest special force in World War II. They were specialists in jungle warfare against the Japanese in Burma. In Operation Longcloth in 1943, they marched more than 1500 kilometres in humid and difficult terrain, far into enemy territory.

28 The US 'Merrill's Marauders' earned their nickname by undertaking an astonishing raid in 1944. Their commander, Brigadier General Frank Merrill, led his men right through Burma to the northern town of Myitkyina to cut a vital railway line and to perform acts of sabotage behind Japanese lines.

▶ Helicopters have become crucial for special forces operating in jungle territory. They can drop a small raiding force deep in the jungle – or pick it up again like this if the going gets tough.

▲ Using only light gear that could be carried on their backs or on mules, Merrill's Marauders used the cover of the Burmese jungle to make daring raids.

29 The Malayan Scouts had incredible survival techniques. It was said that no army patrol could endure jungle terrain for much more than a week, but the Scouts were able to last for months. It is impossible to parachute into thick jungle, so the Scouts pioneered the technique of climbing down ropes into treetops from helicopters.

BRITISH SPECIAL FORCES

30 Britain's special forces come under the umbrella 'UKSF' – United Kingdom Special Forces. They include specialist SAS units trained for reconnaissance and to fight terrorism, and SBS (Special Boat Service) units, which focus on terrorism at sea, and special missions on coasts and in swamps.

▶ The SAS's badge shows a flaming sword in a crusader shield. It was inspired by the British victory at Tobruk in Operation Crusader in World War II.

31 The Air Troop is the parachute division of the SAS. They are also known as the 'Freefall troop', because when dropped into enemy territory they often delay opening their chutes for as long as possible to avoid detection. They have to jump far behind enemy lines, either to undertake missions themselves or to prepare the way for the regular army.

32 The motto of the SAS is 'Who Dares Wins'. The phrase is famous today, but its origins are unknown. Similar phrases appear in the work of ancient Greek playwright Sophocles, and in a letter written by the ancient Roman poet Horace.

◀ The SAS have to be prepared to use tear gas, designed to irritate the eyes and cause difficulty breathing, so may have to wear gas masks.

Heckler & Koch MP5 submachine gun

Respirator

Respirator filter

Bulletproof vest

Leather gloves

33 The SAS carried out a rescue mission on the Iranian embassy in London.

On 30 April, 1980, gunmen entered the embassy and took 26 people hostage. Over the next six days five of the hostages were released. Then one was killed by the terrorists and the government ordered the SAS to take action. SAS soldiers swarmed down ropes from the roof and burst through the windows, guns at the ready. The mission lasted 17 minutes. During this time another hostage was killed by one of the terrorists, but all other hostages were freed and all but one of the gunmen were killed.

▲ The SAS made the headlines when they burst into the Iranian embassy in London in 1980 to rescue hostages from gunmen. The man on the left is an escaping hostage, those on the right are SAS.

34 The Boat Troop is the boat section of the SAS.

They use small inflatable and rigid boats, and their tasks include dropping and picking up special forces soldiers by water, spying underwater, sinking enemy ships, and fighting terrorism at sea. There is a fierce rivalry between the Boat Troop and the sailors of the SBS, but they often go on missions together.

35 The Special Reconnaissance Regiment is a new and secretive special forces unit.

Their main role is to observe and gather information on potentially dangerous people and situations. Their most important task is to keep terrorists under surveillance and they use the latest electronic spying equipment. They are the only special forces unit that admits women.

► The badge of the Special Reconnaissance Regiment shows the helmet of an ancient Greek hoplite soldier and the legendary King Arthur's sword, Excalibur.

▼ The Special Boat Service's new superboat can reach 110 kilometres per hour and avoids radar detection with special 'stealth' technology.

AMERICAN SPECIAL FORCES

36 American special forces units include the Green Berets, Delta Force and SEALs. No outsider knows the full range of units, as some are top-secret. There are even unfounded rumours that there is a special force that relies on telepathy – communication using the power of thought. All US special forces are overseen by the Special Operations Command (SOCOM).

37 The Green Berets specialize in unconventional warfare. This means that they fight more like guerrillas (armed rebel forces) than regular soldiers. Their tactic is to hit targets by surprise in quick raids. The US Army says they work at 'subversion, sabotage, intelligence gathering, escape and evasion'. By this they mean that the role of the Green Berets is to enter enemy territory, create problems, gather information, and get away.

QUICK-FIRE QUIZ

1. How many officers are there in an A-team?
2. What does SOCOM stand for?
3. How many kilometres do Delta Force recruits have to cover in their final training march?

Answers:
1. Two 2. Special Operations Command
3. 64 kilometres

▼ The American Green Berets are trained to cope with the toughest conditions. Here they are training not only to survive in the icy waters of a marsh, but to carry on fighting without tiring.

38 A-teams are key to US special forces. An A-team consists of two officers and ten sergeants. Each team member is chosen and trained to create a broad range of skills across a team, so that every team can operate independently in hostile territory. Different teams specialize in different kinds of mission, from combat diving to mountain warfare.

▶ In the 'Drown Proofing Test', SEAL trainees are dropped into a tank with their hands and feet tied. They have to keep bouncing off the bottom of the tank to surface and catch their breath, until they manage to free themselves and swim to safety.

39 **The US Navy SEALs work mostly on or in water.** Many SEALs are highly trained divers, able to approach tricky targets underwater. In the first Gulf War (1990–1991), a small group of SEALs created a fake attack on the beaches of Kuwait. They succeeded in fooling the Iraqi army into thinking the US attack was coming from the sea.

40 **Delta Force is an elite unit whose task is to combat terrorism, along with the US Navy SEALs.** Delta Force recruits have to endure extremely tough training, similar to that of the British SAS. Training finishes with a gruelling 64-kilometre march across rough terrain, wearing a rucksack that weighs 20 kilograms. Those who complete the march are then subjected to extensive psychological testing.

41 **The Americans insist there are four truths about special forces.** These are: that humans are more important than hardware; that quality is better than quantity; that special operations forces cannot be mass-produced; and that competent special operations forces cannot be created after emergencies occur.

▼ The Search and Rescue team are sent into operations to fly soldiers and airmen to safety. Here they are rehearsing the rescue of a crashed pilot under enemy fire using a CH-53E Super Stallion helicopter.

AROUND THE WORLD

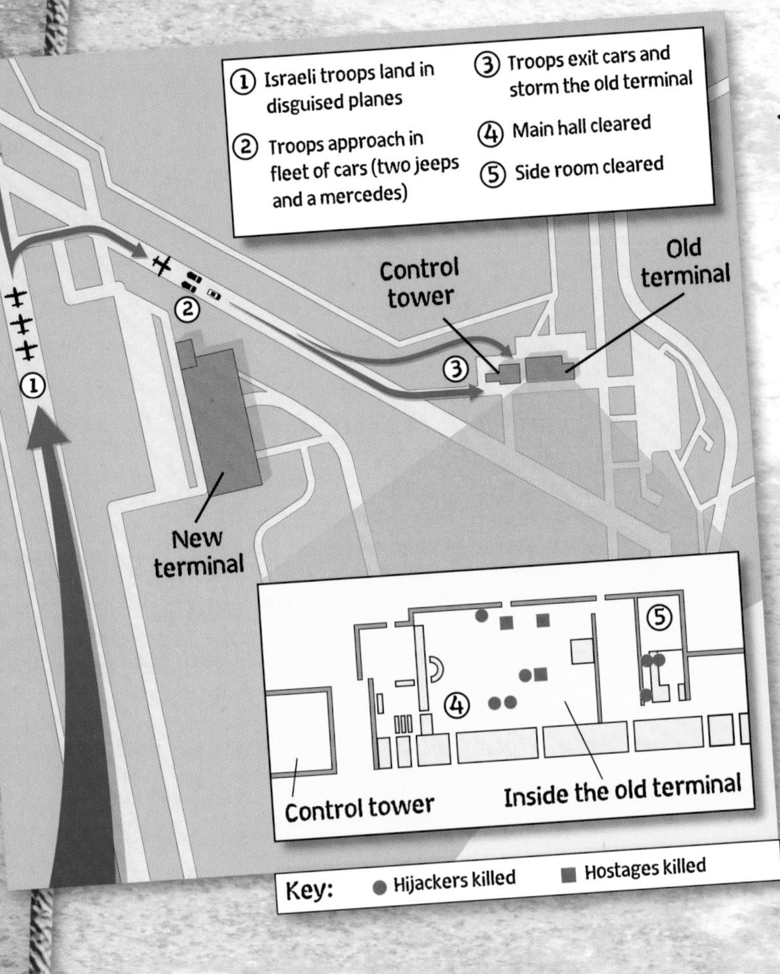

▼ This map shows how the Israeli special forces made their dramatic and mostly successful bid to rescue hostages from Entebbe airport in Uganda.

42 Sayeret Matkal is a unit of the Israeli Defence Force. In July, 1976, hijackers forced an airliner carrying 246 people to land at Entebbe airport in Uganda. They held the hostages at the airport's old terminal. Sayeret Matkal soldiers flew into the airport in disguised planes, and approached the old terminal in a fleet of cars. The hijackers thought the cars were the escort of Ugandan president, Idi Amin, who supported them, so did not react. The operatives killed the hijackers and flew off with the hostages.

43 Russia's key special force is called Spetsnaz. Until 1991 its main role was to spy on and kill enemies of the government. It was also used to fight guerrillas in the mountains of Afghanistan in the 1980s. It is now considered to be one of the world's best counter-terrorist forces.

▶ The Russian Spetsnaz includes some of the world's most accurate and highly trained snipers. Here, a soldier prepares to fire.

A German GSG-9 soldier competes in the World SWAT Challenge to find the world's best special forces.

▲ Sayeret Matkal insignia

44 France's GIGN counter-terrorist force are policemen, not soldiers, but they are famous for their sniping skills. In 1976, a school bus was hijacked in Djibouti, East Africa. The hijackers were allowing food to be sent in for the children, so the GIGN sent sandwiches containing tranquilizers (drugs that send you to sleep). The tranquilized children fell asleep in their seats, giving the GIGN sniper team a clear view to kill the terrorists and rescue the children. Sadly, one little girl was killed too.

45 Australia's main special force is the Special Air Service Regiment (SASR). Inspired by the SAS, they became known as the 'eyes and ears of the Australian Task Force' (the main Australian army) during the Vietnam war (1965–1975). Now its main task is to fight against terrorism.

46 Germany's GSG-9 were formed after a police attempt to rescue a group of athletes taken hostage at the 1972 Munich Olympics went tragically wrong. One of the GSG-9's most famous missions occurred in 1977, when hijackers forced an airliner to fly to Mogadishu, Somalia. While the hijackers were distracted by a fire in front of the plane, GSG-9 soldiers sneaked onto the wings using rubber ladders. Then they burst into the plane and fired stun grenades to knock everyone out. They killed all but one of the terrorists and rescued all the hostages.

Turkish special forces in operation against Kurdish guerrillas, Turkey.

MAKING THE GRADE

47 Recruits to the British SAS are put through a gruelling selection process. Only one applicant out of 12 is successful, even though most are trained soldiers. A potential recruit's first task is to walk 10 kilometres rapidly across country, carrying a rifle and heavy rucksack. And it gets much tougher – applicants are only allowed four hours of sleep before they are sent off on the next task.

48 If someone makes it through the first week of selection, he is sent on Test Week. This ends in the dreaded 'Long Drag', in which applicants march for 60 kilometres over Pen-y-Fan, the highest point in the Brecon Beacons, Wales. The Long Drag must be completed in 20 hours, while carrying a 25-kilogram pack (bergen). It's so tough that men have died trying to complete it. The recruiters say, 'We don't try to fail you, we try to kill you.'

49 To test navigation and map-reading skills, applicants have to find their way to a target through swamps and forest in pitch darkness. No one is permitted to use a Global Positioning System (GPS) – an electronic navigation gadget – and anyone who goes near a road is instantly failed.

▶ Members of the special forces need to be skilled using weapons but also in hand-to-hand fighting. Here, Korean special forces are trained in martial arts.

50

A special forces soldier has to be an expert fighter. Potential recruits have to complete intensive combat training, where they learn skills such as hand-to-hand combat and fighting with a knife. The standards demanded are very high, and anyone who fails to make the grade is kicked out.

51

The toughest part of the SAS selection process is jungle training in Brunei, Southeast Asia. Applicants are sent into the jungle in groups of four. They have to spend two weeks hacking through thick undergrowth and wading through swamps in soaring temperatures. During jungle training potential recruits may have to contend with dangerous animals and poisonous plants. Many have to be rescued.

52

In the final test, applicants have to live off the land for seven days while evading capture by pursuing soldiers. No one has yet succeeded completely. When caught, applicants are submitted to hours of gruelling interrogation. Finally, they are rescued by their colleagues. This test is called Survive, Evade, Resist, Extract (SERE).

TRAINING FOR ACTION

53 Fitness is a big part of special forces training. Recruits train to build strength and go on long marches to increase endurance. Even before selection, applicants must be able to do 40 push-ups in two minutes and run 12.8 kilometres in two hours, while carrying a 21-kilogram pack and a 4-kilogram rifle!

▲ Submachine guns such as the old Heckler & Koch MP5 are key weapons.

▶ Stun grenades are used to knock enemies out for vital seconds while an attack is made.

54 A recruit has to master a range of weapons. These include specialist equipment for use in hostage-rescue missions. Soldiers learn to use items such as stun grenades, tear gas, explosives and shotguns.

55 The 'Killing House' sounds like the name of a horror film, but it is actually part of British SAS training. The US Green Berets' version is called the 'House of Horrors'. It is a purpose-built house for use in training special forces soldiers to rescue hostages. The walls inside are moveable, and walls and doors are coated in rubber to absorb gunfire safely. There are fans to take out gun smoke, and a variety of traps can be set to catch operatives if they do not follow correct procedures.

A training raid on a house in complete darkness using night vision equipment.

56 Special forces soldiers must be able to mount an attack on any target, from a skyscraper to a plane. Exceptional climbing skills are essential so that soldiers can enter buildings by climbing up a wall or abseiling (speeding down on a rope) from the roof.

New recruits practise 'tubular assaults' – training on mock-ups of tube-shaped vehicles in preparation for potential hostage situations on planes, trains and buses.

◀ A member of Bangkok's special commando unit dives off the top of a building during a training exercise. He holds a tool for breaking windows and his gun at the ready.

Often, establishing a good relationship with locals is as important as fighting. Here a US soldier hands out crayons in Afghanistan.

57 Throughout training, special forces soldiers work on their language skills. Missions may take them to foreign countries, or require international cooperation. Soldiers working abroad may have to give instructions to civilians, or ask them for information, or simply establish good relations with the local population. Any problems with language could be disastrous, so teams often include members fluent in a range of languages.

TACTICS AND TECHNIQUES

58 Four is the best number of men for a small patrol. Smaller patrols move faster and can hide more easily, but you need at least four people to carry the necessary supplies and equipment. Having four people also means that if one of the group is injured, two people can carry him while the fourth keeps watch.

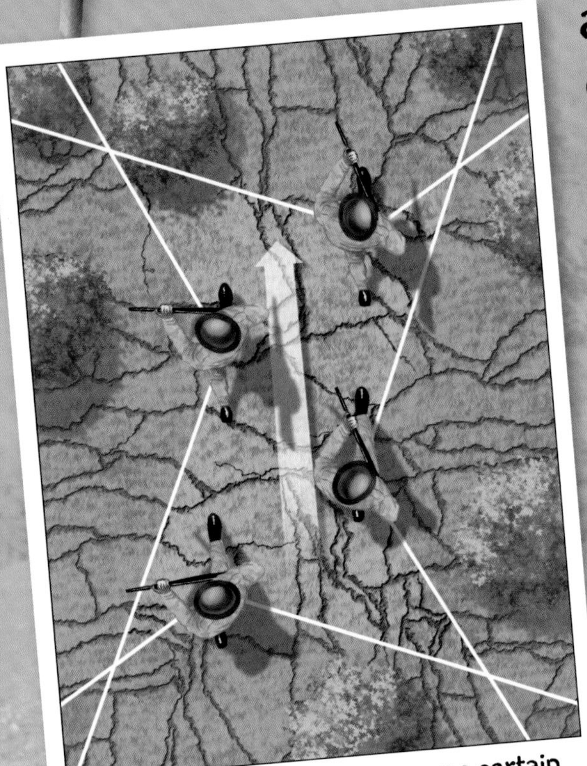

Each patrol member must cover a certain area with his gun.

59 To ensure protection from all directions, each soldier covers an angle of visibility with his gun. The last man ('tailend charlie'), is usually armed with a machine gun to provide covering fire in case of attack from behind. Every 30 minutes, the soldiers lie down to form a circle with each person facing outwards. They observe their surroundings, listening intently for any sound that suggests they are being followed. This is called 'all-round defence'.

60 A patrol is most likely to be attacked at dawn. Darkness just before dawn provides cover for enemy soldiers to creep close, and sunrise gives enough visibility to launch an attack. Patrols need to be ready to move just before dawn. Then they 'stand to' for 30 minutes, watching carefully with weapons ready. When the sun is up and all is clear they can move off.

▲ A routine four-man foot patrol by Turkish commandos in the mountains on the Turkish border.

▲ Royal Marines of 45 Commando patrol for enemy soldiers in the mountains of southeastern Afghanistan.

CODE CONUNDRUM

Can you unscramble the letters below to make some key special forces terms?

1. TRAPLO 2. SHUMBA
3. TINDALE REALHIC
4. KATACT 5. YEMEN RIFE

Answers:
1. Patrol 2. Ambush
3. Tailend charlie 4. Attack
5. Enemy fire

61 Patrol members are trained to act instantly if ambushed. If a patrol is under attack in an area where taking cover isn't an option, soldiers must try to dodge the first bursts of enemy fire and run straight forwards, over the top of the enemy. This kind of quick reaction has saved the lives of many ambushed special forces soldiers.

62 Patrols memorize tactics so they can react instantly. The patrol commander is in charge, but in tricky situations there may not be time to issue orders. Soldiers are trained to know what to do in potential crises without being told. Every unit has its own book of tactics, or 'Standard Operating Procedures', which soldiers have to memorize, as any hesitation or mistake could be fatal.

63 Setting up a perfect ambush (surprise attack) may take weeks. Good locations have plenty of cover, and few escape routes for the target. Patrols may lay mines to cause the target to stop at a certain point, where soldiers are placed in position to prevent the target escaping. A central 'killer' group launches the main attack. Either side of this, support groups provide cover and surround the target. A flanking group prevents attack from the rear.

▼ Learning how to defend yourself effectively against an ambush, called 'ground defence', is a vital part of training for special forces patrols.

64 Every special forces soldier learns navigation skills. Today, the SAS exploits global navigation technology such as GPS, which uses satellite signals to pinpoint the user's location. However, some situations may require more old-fashioned skills such as map-reading or navigating by the position of the stars.

▲ Special forces are expected to be able to find their way across open country using just a map and a compass to guide them.

65 Special forces soldiers have to be prepared to perform difficult tasks in severe weather conditions. An operation may require them to cross an icy mountain range during a blizzard, or trek for days through a humid tropical rainforest. To survive such extremes of climate, soldiers have to be physically fit and well prepared. Having the right clothing and equipment may be the difference between life and death.

▶ Fish may be a vital source of fresh food in the wild, so a simple fishing kit can be a life-saver.

66 In icy conditions, warm clothing is essential. Soldiers have to try to keep their clothes as dry as possible, because heat escapes more easily from wet clothing. A tent or makeshift shelter is vital for surviving a night in freezing temperatures. Cold winds and sweating from skiing or marching can cause dehydration (insufficient water in the body), so soldiers take fuel to melt snow for water.

▼ A combat survival kit containing: button compass (1), candle (2), flint and striker (3), knife (4), book of matches (5), sewing kit (6), whistle (7), snare wire (8), water purification tablets (9), wire saw (10).

67 **If a soldier is alone and far from base, he may have to live off the land.** In this situation, rations (supplies of food and drink) may run out, or have to be made to last for longer than was planned. Soldiers research the plant life in the region of their mission so that they can identify edible wild plants. It is possible to survive for ten days or more without much food, but humans need fresh water daily.

▶ The soldier's backpack is his life support system. It allows him to carry all he needs for a long mission, leaving his arms free.

68 **A soldier going on patrol in difficult terrain takes a survival kit.** This typically includes items such as a wire saw for cutting wood, thin wire for making snares to catch animals to eat, basic fishing gear, a flint to light a fire, a candle, a knife, a first aid kit and a compass.

ON THE ATTACK

69 During wartime, the main task of special forces is sabotage. This means sneaking into enemy territory to attack key points, such as railway lines. During the first Gulf War, SAS forces were used to sabotage Iraqi radio masts. Under the cover of darkness, armed trucks moved into position as a 'fire support group' (FSG). Meanwhile, an assault team stuck explosives to the masts. The Iraqi guards were alerted, but too late to act. The FSG provided covering fire as the assault team detonated the explosives and retreated.

▼ A view through a telescopic sight.

70 Soldiers are trained to use explosives, but each patrol also has a demolitions expert. The type of device used to trigger a bomb depends on the situation. Sometimes a bomb can be set off from a distance using a radio-controlled firing device or an electronic trigger. At other times, soldiers simply light a fuse on the bomb itself before retreating quickly to a safe distance.

A sniper often works with a spotter, who keeps watch while the sniper lines up his telescopic site on the target.

▲ Staying hidden is crucial for a sniper. Here snipers are camouflaged pretty effectively as bushes in misty marshland.

71 Snipers are trained to shoot accurately over a long range, from a concealed location. They can hit a target up to one kilometre away, and may have to stalk a target for days before making a shot. To avoid being spotted, snipers wear camouflage, and choose their hiding places carefully.

72 A sniper rifle has a long, heavy barrel so that bullets leave it on the straightest possible path. It also has a telescopic (magnifying) or laser-guided sight for greater accuracy. A sniper rifle is not carried slung on the shoulder, but in a case. This also contains other equipment such as mounts to increase the gun's stability when making a shot.

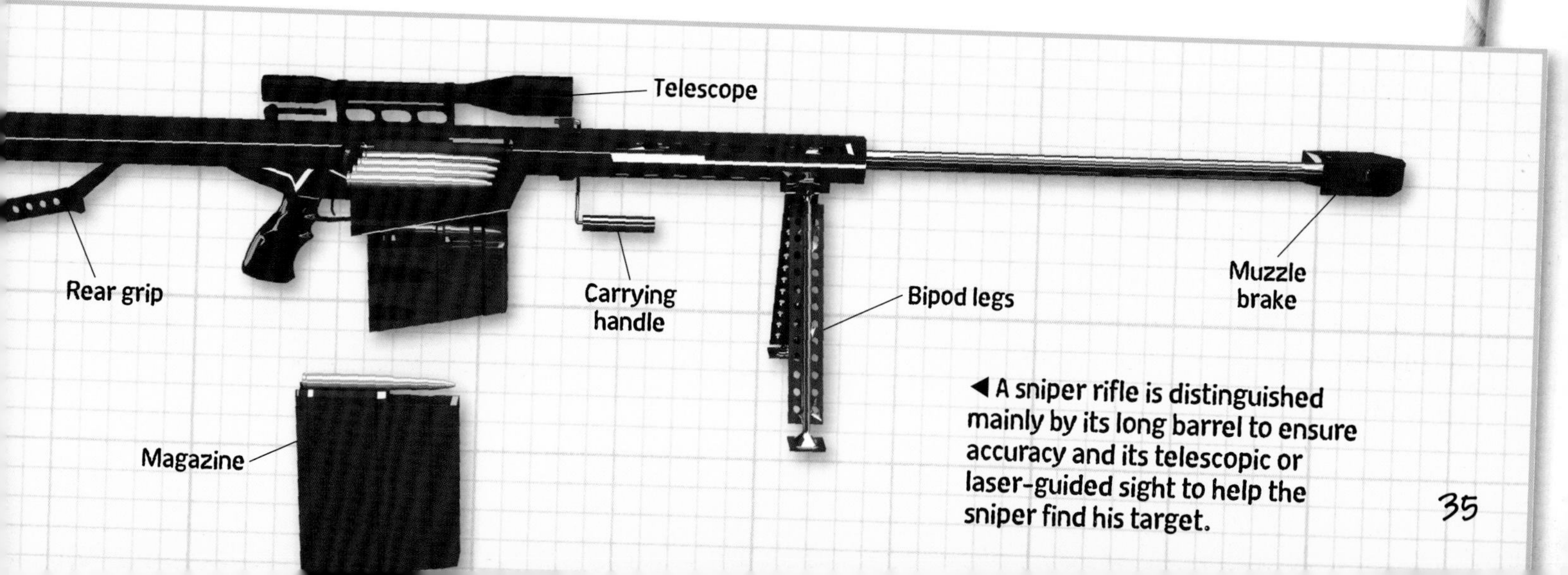

◀ A sniper rifle is distinguished mainly by its long barrel to ensure accuracy and its telescopic or laser-guided sight to help the sniper find his target.

COUNTERING TERRORISM

73 Fighting terrorism is the main task of special forces outside of wartime. This is called 'counter-terrorism'. Terrorists are people who try to make governments or communities do what they want by using violence, such as taking people hostage or blowing up buildings.

▶ Hostages often need to be rescued from inside buildings. It's a dangerous situation and special forces train hard to make an attack with minimum casualties.

74 The police may be able to prevent acts of terrorism before they happen. They try to gather information about potential terrorists by keeping them under surveillance (observation). However, terrorists may act before the police can catch them. That's when special forces are called in.

75 If terrorists take hostages, special forces have to move fast. If the hostages are being held inside a building, snipers move into position around it to observe the situation and wait for a signal to act. The snipers work in pairs, sending a stream of information back to command. In the British SAS, snipers call terrorists 'X-rays' and hostages 'Yankees'.

76 When negotiations fail or hostages are in immediate danger, a direct attack may be needed.

Sometimes, 'assaulters' creep in quietly to catch the terrorists by surprise. But if the situation is urgent, they may have to 'go noisy'. That means bursting in quickly, blowing open doors with explosives and throwing stun grenades to overwhelm the terrorists before they have a chance to react.

77 Piracy is a new threat for special forces to deal with.

There are now pirates in Somalia, on the coast of East Africa, who go out in small boats and attack passing ships. In April 2009, the American captain of the container ship *Maersk Alabama* was kidnapped by pirates. US Navy SEAL special forces raced in and rescued him, killing three of the pirates.

▲ French special forces are seen here in January 2009 capturing 19 Somali pirates before they could make their attack on a ship in the Gulf of Aden.

RAIDING BY WATER

78 Divers are key in some special forces operations. Approaching underwater is a good way to pass unseen into enemy territory. Shipping, port facilities and oil rigs are all possible targets for terrorists. Combat divers often have to operate in cold, dark water, and are trained to cope with awkward obstacles and other hazards.

▼ US Navy SEALs burst from the sea in diving suits, guns at the ready for a surprise attack from the water.

79 Combat divers should never have to swim far during a mission. Swimming is slow and exhausting, so divers are dropped off as close to their target as possible. To avoid detection, they travel by submarine first. Then light, inflatable boats are launched in the darkness to take them closer.

▼ A US Navy SEAL, dressed in scuba gear, carries waterproof weapons including a submachine gun, a depth gauge, and an underwater bomb while training.

80 Special forces divers use rebreathers to avoid creating bubbles on the surface of the water. A rebreather is a device that traps the diver's breath and re-circulates it so that air bubbles don't escape, and give away the diver's position. Equipment of this kind is complex and potentially dangerous, so using it requires a high level of training.

▲ A special forces diver gets ready to launch his own Swimmer Delivery Vehicle underwater from a submarine. The SDV is 'wet', and the diver will sit astride it to ride to the target.

81 Many combat divers use Swimmer Delivery Vehicles (SDVs). These are small submersibles for the transport of combat divers. There are two kinds of SDV – 'wet', where the diver sits astride the SDV exposed to the water, or 'dry', where the diver sits inside. Midget (small) submarines are used for longer missions. Many of these submersibles use stealth technology, which shields them from detection by absorbing or reflecting sonar waves.

82 Small rubber inflatable boats are useful in all kinds of situations. They can be dropped from a helicopter to inflate automatically when they hit the water, or inflated on the decks of submarines. They can be powered by a small outboard motor, or paddled when stealth is needed.

83 A 'Rigid Inflatable Boat' (RIB) has a rigid glass-reinforced plastic (GRP) base to keep its shape. An inflatable tube rim keeps it afloat even if it is swamped by waves. RIBs are much faster and more controllable than small inflatables, but they can't be packed up and dropped so easily from a helicopter or submarine.

▼ Fast and light, rigid inflatable boats (RIBs) are vital for getting small attack groups ashore quickly from ships.

DROPPING FROM THE AIR

84 The quickest way to get soldiers into position in difficult territory is by parachute. Paratroopers can be whisked to the furthest corners of the globe and dropped into place in a matter of hours – silently and under cover of darkness if need be. But parachuting can be very dangerous – especially at night and into rugged terrain.

By parachute, special forces can drop literally out of the blue into enemy territory, but they need to hit their targets accurately.

85 Sometimes paratroopers go HAHO. This stands for High Altitude High Opening. It means jumping from the plane so high up it can't be seen from the ground, then opening the chute quickly. Modern chutes can be steered by pulling on toggles to glide down slowly over 40 kilometres further on. This way, forces can penetrate deeper into enemy territory than a plane might safely take them. However it is less accurate, and soldiers might get separated from their group on the way down.

▶ In a high-altitude drop a paratrooper needs to wear an oxygen mask to breathe.

To maximize chances of landing together, paratroopers often begin their drop holding hands in free fall before opening their chutes.

86 Sometimes paratroopers go HALO. This stands for High Altitude Low Opening. It means they will exit the plane at high altitude, then free fall almost to the ground, only opening their chutes at the last minute. Using this method, forces are unlikely to be spotted by an enemy on their way down. Sometimes a group of soldiers may hold hands as they free fall in a 'linked descent' so that they all land in the same drop area.

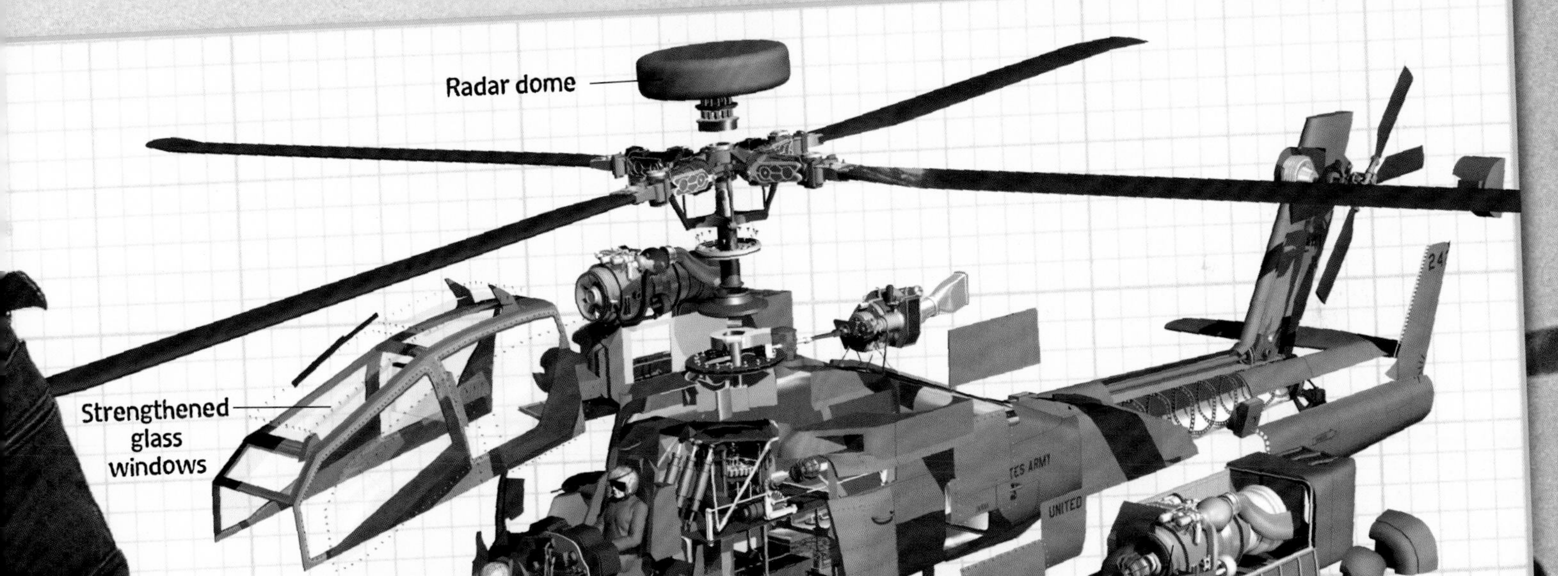

87 Helicopters are the most important form of transport for special forces. They can whisk men and equipment deep inside enemy territory, then pick them up when the mission is complete. Helicopters can also provide vital covering fire for patrols under attack on the ground, and airlift the wounded to safety.

▲ Attack helicopters such as the AH-64 Apache can provide vital firepower and support for troops on the ground.

STAYING IN TOUCH

88 A GPS works by electronically comparing the signals from at least four satellites. With a small hand-held receiver, the user can plot his position to within one metre. In the first Gulf War, US special forces used this technology to guide their tanks into position across the desert, something the Iraqi forces had thought would be impossible.

◀ Laptop computers and telecommunications equipment help special forces locate targets.

89 It is vital that soldiers stay in close personal contact during missions. Every man in a patrol has a digital radio system, allowing him to stay in constant communication with the other members of his team. An earpiece and mouthpiece keeps his hands free. Ordinary soldiers usually only have one radio set per unit, because too much radio traffic can cause confusion, but for special forces, personal radios are vital.

90 A radio signal might give away your position, so modern military radios automatically 'frequency hop' during transmission. This means they continuously change the frequency of the radio waves, making it hard for any eavesdropper to intercept the signal and track the source. Messages are automatically put in code, too, so even if an eavesdropper does pick it up, it's impossible to understand!

◀ The Land Warrior Integrated Fighting System has a helmet display that continually shows the wearer his own location, and that of the enemy.

91 Special forces often guide missiles to their targets. They sneak into enemy territory and pinpoint key objectives, such as missile launch sites. There they set up a piece of equipment called a ground laser target designator. This aims a laser beam at the target and 'paints' it. Computer-guided 'smart' missiles can then see the target and aim for it with pinpoint precision.

▶ This soldier is using a Guidance Laser Illumination Device (GLID) to paint a target with laser light, which will guide attacking aircraft onto it with pinpoint precision.

INTO THE FUTURE

92 **Batwings are jet-powered personal wings made of carbon-fibre.** A person wearing them can be dropped from a plane to fly at low-level for hundreds of kilometres. In 2003, Austrian Felix Baumgartner donned batwings and jumped from a plane at an altitude of 10,000 metres over England, landing in France 12 minutes later. However if special forces are using them, they are keeping it secret.

▶ Could special forces soldiers use batwings like these worn by Felix Baumgartner as he glides across the English Channel in 2003?

▶ The Future Force Warrior suit may look like something out of science fiction, but soldiers are already trying it out.

93 **The American Future Force warrior system will turn a soldier into superman as soon as he puts on his uniform.** In his helmet, electronic links will tell him his exact location and that of the enemy, as well as what to do at all times. Sensors on his body will relay information back to base to tell medics instantly if he is tired or injured. His liquid body armour will be flexible and easy to move around in – but will turn into rigid protection in a thousandth of a second. An 'exoskeleton' of hydraulic arms attached to his real limbs will give him superhuman strength.

TRUE OR FALSE?

1. Felix Baumgartner flew from Spain to France on carbon-fibre wings.
2. Robots can be used to find unexploded bombs.
3. Robots locate snipers by making a chemical analysis of the air.

Answers:
1. False – he flew from England to France
2. True 3. False – they locate them by finding the location of the gunshot

94 **Human soldiers may one day be replaced by robot warriors for some tasks.** The iRobot Warrior looks more like a cartoon tank than a soldier. But it can find unexploded bombs, clear mines and explosives, and even go on reconnaissance missions.

95 **Robots can be used instead of soldiers in some tricky situations.** One type of PackBot is used in Iraq to detect bombs. It finds them by making a chemical analysis of the air. Another kind can locate snipers by pinpointing the direction of the sound of the gunshot.

▼ Remotely operated robots are already performing certain tasks such as bomb detection.

FACT AND FICTION

96 Kit Carson was a real person, but many of the stories told about him are myths. Carson was a scout in the US cavalry in the early 1800s, who in 1842 helped guide a man called John Fremont to Oregon and California. Fremont wrote accounts of the journey that made Carson sound capable of superhuman feats. He became a national hero.

PLUCK AND LUCK
COMPLETE STORIES OF ADVENTURE.

No. 181. NEW YORK, NOVEMBER 20, 1901.

THE BOY RIFLE RANGERS
OR, KIT CARSON'S THREE YOUNG SCOUTS.
BY AN OLD SCOUT.

▶ The cover of a 'Pluck and Luck' book featuring a fictional story about the famous Kit Carson.

▶ A scene from the movie *Black Hawk Down*, which is based on the true story of a mission to rescue the crew of a Black Hawk helicopter shot down in Somalia in 1993.

97 When Lord Robert Baden-Powell created the Boy Scouts in 1907, he was inspired by stories. Baden-Powell was the hero of the siege of Mafeking (1899–1900) in the Boer War (1899–1902). He got ideas for the Scouts from seeing the Lovat Scouts in action, and from his friend, writer Rudyard Kipling. 'Kim's game' is an exercise for improving observation by memorizing objects on a tray. Baden-Powell got it from Kipling's story of Kim, the orphan hero of his novel of the same name, set in India.

▶ Founder of the Boy Scouts, Robert Baden-Powell was inspired by Kipling's story of Kim.

QUICK-FIRE QUIZ

1. What was Kit Carson's job in the US cavalry?
2. Where is the movie *Black Hawk Down* set?
3. Who wrote the novel *Kim*?

Answers:
1. He was a scout 2. Somalia
3. Rudyard Kipling

98 The most famous exploit of special forces in World War II was a daring raid in Norway. The soldiers were dropped in Norway, and they skied across country to destroy a factory making a special kind of liquid that the Germans might have used to make nuclear weapons. The story became the inspiration for a film about a similar raid called *The Heroes of Telemark* (1965).

99 *The Guns of Navarone* (1961) is a film about a fictional World War II raid on a German fortress on a Greek island. In it, the fortress is destroying Allied shipping in the Aegean Sea, but is thought to be impossible to attack. Commandos launch a daring raid to destroy its deadly guns. This story is entirely fictional and based on a novel by the writer Alistair Maclean.

100 *Black Hawk Down* (2001) is a film about an American special forces mission in Mogadishu, Somalia in 1993. It is about a raid that really happened. The aim of the raid was to capture a Somali warlord, Mohamed Farrah Aidid. During the raid, one of the force's Black Hawk helicopters was shot down. American troops invaded to rescue the stranded soldiers. They succeeded, but only after a ferocious battle.

INDEX

Entries in **bold** refer to main subject entries.
Entries in *italics* refer to illustrations.